DATE DUE		
APR 2 2 2005			

Derek Jeter

Michael Bradley

BENCHMARK BOOKS

MARSHALL CAVENDISH
NEW YORK

Benchmark Books
Marshall Cavendish
99 White Plains Road
Tarrytown, NY 10591-9001
www.marshallcavendish.com

Library of Congress Cataloging-in-Publication Data

Bradley, Michael, 1962-
Derek Jeter / by Michael Bradley.
p. cm. — (Benchmark All-stars)
Summary: Details the rise of Derek Jeter through the minor leagues and
his subsequent seasons with the New York Yankees.
Includes bibliographical references and index.
ISBN 0-7614-1626-9
1. Jeter, Derek, 1974—Juvenile literature. 2. Baseball
players—United States--Biography—Juvenile literature. [1. Jeter,
Derek, 1974- 2. Baseball players. 3. Racially mixed people—Biography.]
I. Title. II. Series.

GV865.J48B73 2004
796.357'092--dc21

2003000740

Series design by Becky Terhune

Printed in Italy
1 3 5 6 4 2

★ Contents

Chapter One | The King of New York 7

Chapter Two | A Star Is Born 13

Chapter Three | The Long Road 19

Chapter Four | In the Big Leagues 25

Chapter Five | Superstardom 31

Chapter Six | Above and Beyond 37

Player Statistics 42

Glossary 44

Find Out More 45

Index 46

Derek Jeter celebrates the New York Yankees' playoff win over Seattle, which clinched a spot in the 2001 World Series.

CHAPTER ONE
The King of New York

The New York Yankees were in trouble. Big trouble. Two quick losses to the Oakland Athletics in the best-of-five first round of the 2001 playoffs had put the **dynasty** in jeopardy. One more defeat, and the dream of a fourth straight World Series title would be gone. With the next two games in northern California—the A's home—things didn't look good for the Bronx Bombers.

New York sent Mike Mussina to the pitcher's mound for the third game, and that offered some encouragement to Yankee fans. "Moose" had won seventeen games for the Yanks during the regular season. The A's wouldn't get much off him. Sure enough, Mussina was marvelous. He entered the seventh **inning** with a 1–0 lead, courtesy of a fifth-inning home run by catcher Jorge Posada. But there was trouble brewing. With two outs, Oakland's Jeremy Giambi singled. Terrence Long followed with a liner to the right-field corner. Giambi, running on contact, was almost certain to score. Almost.

It was Derek Jeter time.

The Yankees' **shortstop,** known for his smooth, graceful manner and for getting hits and making plays in the field in pressure situations, made a play that will be talked about by

Few shortstops in all of baseball can field the position as smoothly as Derek Jeter.

Yankees fans—and anybody who loves baseball—for generations. New York right fielder Shane Spencer's throw to the plate was off-line. As Giambi steamed for home, Jeter cruised from his position on the left side of the infield to the first-base line, where he intercepted the wayward toss and backhanded the ball to Posada. In one motion, Posada caught the ball and swept it behind him, nicking Giambi's foot

before it could hit the plate. Inning over. Threat ended. Jeter saves the day. New York won, 1–0, and captured the next two games to take the series from the stunned A's.

"It was the play of the game," New York manager Joe Torre said afterward. "[Jeter's] the backup *cutoff man* in that situation. He was there, and he made a sensational play. He has great instincts. He holds it together."

Nearby, Jeter held court. In his trademark laid-back style, he deflected praise from himself and focused on the importance of the win. According to Jeter, he had done nothing special; he had just helped the Yankees win.

"That's my job, and I did it," he said. "I have to move forward on that play. If I had spun around, I wouldn't have made it. I didn't think [Giambi] had a chance to score when it was first hit."

He didn't score, thanks to Derek Jeter. Once again, the young Yankee had proved himself to be one of baseball's best players. In big situations, stars step up. Jeter may not be comfortable recognizing himself as an elite player, but there can be no questioning what he means to his team, and to baseball. In just six full seasons, Jeter has played on four *World Series* championship teams, been named to four *American League* All-Star teams, and assumed the role of leader on what is arguably America's most famous sporting franchise, the New York Yankees. An indication of that can be found on his uniform. He wears the number 2, one of just a pair of single-digit numerals that haven't been retired by the Yankees. By the time Jeter retires, his jersey will be off-limits for future Yanks, too.

It is like a dream come true for the 6′ 3″ (190 centimeter), 195-pound (88-kilogram) shortstop. Jeter spent part of his childhood in New Jersey and grew up rooting for the Yankees and his hero, outfielder Dave Winfield. And now he's wearing the pin-stripes. Sometimes dreams do come true.

Jeter has a style and elegance that are unparalleled in sports. He smiles for the cameras, signs autographs willingly for his fans, and is smooth with the media. His appeal crosses genders and cultural and

Jeter displays his winning smile and his four World Series championship rings.

Jeter is cheered on by thousands of fans, and he is always willing to meet them.

economic lines. More than 6,000 Derek Jeter Web sites exist. He has hosted *Saturday Night Live*, a popular late-night television comedy show. He receives loud ovations on the road. For many fans, Jeter represents the total package.

"Culturally, he appeals to a wide range of people," former Yankees pitcher David Cone told the New York *Daily News* in 2000. "Everywhere you go there are Derek Jeter fans. He makes us into a sort of traveling show in every town we go to. He embodies everything that's good about the game right now, and he's a young superstar. He can carry the game."

Jeter doesn't seek out such responsibility, but he doesn't shy

> "He embodies everything that's good about the game right now, and he's a young superstar."
> —David Cone

away from it, either. Despite his relative youth, Jeter is the leader of the Yankees' team. His style isn't to be a cheerleader, but rather a steady force on the field and in the clubhouse. Teammates can count on his support, and can also expect his anger to show on occasion, too. But it's all done quietly, confidently. Jeter is about winning. That's why he made the big play in Oakland, and countless others like it. That's why he is considered the future of the franchise. That's why he's a star.

It's great to be young and a champion in New York!

There's Only One!

Whether it's practice or a game, Jeter always prepares to do his best.

CHAPTER TWO

A Star Is Born

Derek Jeter's favorite team was always the Yankees. Even after Jeter and his family moved away from West Milford, New Jersey, which is just a long relay throw from New York City, he dreamed of wearing the pinstripes and playing in Yankee Stadium. Jeter had a poster of Dave Winfield on his bedroom wall. He wore a Yankees cap, necklace, and jacket.

"When he was in Little League, he said he was going to play for the Yankees," his father, Charles Jeter, said.

Dreams cannot be guaranteed. In order to come true, they often need hard work and a lot of luck. Jeter had plenty of the former and a little of the latter.

He was born on June 26, 1974, in New Jersey. His family moved to Kalamazoo, Michigan, when Derek was four, but he and his sister, Sharlee, would spend part of their summers visiting their grandparents, William and Dot Connors, back in Jersey. Derek would play ball with Dot, talk baseball, and root for the Yankees. Dot had cheered for the Yanks since the days when Joe DiMaggio patrolled center field and the team seemed to win the World Series every year. She had even gone to Yankee Stadium back in 1948, a few days after the great Babe Ruth's death, and walked past the Bambino's casket with thousands of other mourning fans.

Jeter has become a better and more powerful hitter since coming to the major leagues.

On those summer mornings, Derek would awake before anybody else and play catch with Dot. "All his cousins would still be sleeping, and he would say, 'C'mon, Gram, let's throw,'" Dot Connors told *Sports Illustrated* in 1996. "He wanted to be a pitcher then. I was his catcher. Even as a little kid, his throw would almost knock me over."

Derek was a talented player, earning spots in Little League all-star games and displaying talent on the basketball court, too. But life was not all sports for Derek. His parents, Charles and Dorothy Jeter, demanded much more of their children. Both had earned college degrees and achieved plenty in their professions. Charles Jeter was a drug and alcohol counselor, and Dorothy Jeter was an accountant. Each fall, Derek's parents made him sign a contract that laid out their expectations. He was to study every day, make straight As on his report cards, avoid drugs and alcohol, observe an early curfew, finish his chores without any argument, treat others with respect, and refrain from talking about himself. It was a demanding set of requirements, but Jeter realizes now how much his parents' rules helped him.

"If you want me to brag, ask me about my parents," he once said.

> **"When he was in Little League, he said he was going to play for the Yankees."**
> **—Charles Jeter**

Jeter faced another challenge, beyond the classroom, home, or on the baseball diamond. Charles Jeter is African American; Dorothy Jeter is Irish American. Derek and Sharlee couldn't have cared less about that. Others weren't always so understanding. Some said nasty things or stayed away from the Jeter children because of their biracial status. It wasn't always easy, but they rose above the prejudice and hate.

"People sometimes said things, but my feeling was always 'Why let an ignorant person bother me?'" Jeter said. "Growing up, I had friends who were black, white and Hispanic. I was surrounded by so many good people, I never had much of a problem. My parents, I'm sure, had to deal with a lot more than I did. They made it all easy for me."

How to Figure Out a Batting Average

Derek Jeter counts his father, Charles, among his greatest inspirations.

⭐ Cooperstown's Hall of Fame

By the time he reached high school, Derek was thriving in every way possible. He was an A student and a star shortstop at Kalamazoo Central. Derek hit .557 as a junior and .508 as a senior. The American Baseball Coaches Association named Derek its 1992 High School Player of the Year. Professional scouts and college coaches flocked to his games. Derek signed a letter-of-intent to attend the University of Michigan, but he was still dreaming of the Yankees.

Unfortunately, it didn't appear that the club was dreaming about him. Scouts from twenty-seven of the twenty-eight major-league teams made the trip to Kalamazoo and contacted Jeter. The Yankees were the only team to refrain. As the 1992 amateur draft approached, it appeared as if the Cincinnati Reds would select Jeter, with the fifth overall pick. In the draft, teams select players in rounds. Jeter was the fifth pick in the first round, therefore the fifth overall pick. Jeter's favorite player, Barry Larkin, was the Reds' shortstop, and Jeter feared he would be a long-time backup behind the Cincinnati native. Still, because he had been taught not to complain, Jeter began to envision himself wearing a Cincinnati uniform.

> **"If you want me to brag, ask me about my parents."**
> **—Derek Jeter**

Two days before the draft, Dick Groch, a Yankees scout, called the Jeter home. He said the team had been following Jeter for two years, but had refrained from calling on him out of respect for the family's privacy. Jeter was thrilled, but still uncertain. What if the Reds had chosen him for the draft? He would have to wait. As it turned out, the Yankees were as anxious to have Jeter as he was to join him. Groch was clear in his assessment of Jeter. When the Yankees wondered whether Jeter would attend the University of Michigan, rather than join the club immediately if it drafted him, Groch had no doubts. "There's only one place Derek Jeter's going for sure," he said. "Cooperstown."

On draft day, Cincinnati announced it would select outfielder Chad Mottola, a proven college player from the University of Central Florida. The Yankees were up next, and made their choice—Jeter. He would be playing for his favorite team, with a shot at standing on the field at the hallowed Yankee Stadium. "It was a freak happening," Jeter said.

Or a dream come true.

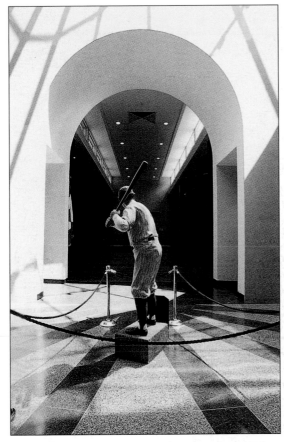

The Baseball Hall of Fame is filled with hundreds of interesting exhibits, like this statue of Yankees great Babe Ruth.

> **"There's only one place Derek Jeter's going for sure Cooperstown."**
> **—Dick Groch**

As a boy, Derek Jeter cheered for the New York Yankees. Now he is one of them!

CHAPTER THREE
The Long Road

Derek Jeter had been drafted by the Yankees. He had signed a contract with the Yankees.

But he wasn't a Yankee yet.

The road to the majors almost always includes some time in the minor leagues. New York thought Jeter would be a star, its shortstop of the future. But even that wouldn't keep him from paying his dues. His first stop was Tampa's Gulf Coast League. He was on the rookie circuit.

It wasn't exactly a triumphant performance. Jeter played forty-seven games in the 1992 season and hit a mere .202, striking out just about every fifth time he went to the plate. He made twenty-one errors. Naturally, he was heartbroken. He called home so often that his long-distance bills were enormous. Sure, he had the red sports car he had bought with his first paycheck, but Jeter wondered if he had made the right decision. Maybe he should have gone to the University of Michigan and gained some seasoning. Maybe he wasn't going to play in Yankee Stadium after all.

"I cried in my room every night," Jeter said. "I'd never been away from home before, and

No stadium in baseball history has hosted as many great moments as Yankee Stadium.

I didn't feel like I belonged. I felt overmatched."

Jeter was upset, but the Yankees knew they had a diamond in the rough. Instead of giving up on him, they promoted Jeter, warts and all. He spent the last two weeks of the year at the Yankees' Class A affiliate in Greensboro, North Carolina. It was still miles from the Bronx, the home of Yankee Stadium, but it represented a step forward, nonetheless. The Yankees had faith in him.

It showed in early 1993. The Yankees have a long-standing tradition of inviting first-round picks to the big club's spring training in Fort Lauderdale, Florida. Jeter was still a minor-league puppy, miles from the big time, but he was sharing the clubhouse and the diamond with his heroes.

"I'm nineteen and throwing to (former Yankees first baseman) Don Mattingly," Jeter said. "I'm going from Kalamazoo Central High School, with a friend of mine at third and another friend of mine at first, and here I am at spring training,

> **"I'd never been away from home before, and I didn't feel like I belonged."**
> **—Derek Jeter**

Jeter worked hard in the minor leagues to improve his fielding.

with Wade Boggs (former Yankee third baseman), to my right, and I'm throwing to Don Mattingly. I couldn't believe it."

The six-week session was a tremendous learning experience for Jeter. Even though he would be returning to Greensboro, he was getting a dose of the big time. He was also spending time with consummate professionals, like Boggs and Mattingly. One day, Mattingly gave him some valuable advice. Jeter and Mattingly had finished working out and were on their way back to the clubhouse. The training complex was empty, but Mattingly told Jeter to run in anyway. "You never know who's watching," Mattingly said.

It was a simple lesson, but one Jeter never forgot. It's important to hustle, important to show fans, the media, or just even the grounds crew how much you love the game, how much you want to be great. "There were no fans, no coaches, no media around," Jeter said. "Nobody was watching. That made a big impression on me. Since that day, when I'm on the field, I always run."

Running wasn't the problem. Fielding was. Jeter played the entire 1993 campaign in Greensboro, hitting .295, with 5 homers, 14 doubles, and 11 triples. He stole 18 bases. But he continued to struggle in the field, making a whopping 56 errors in 126

The Minor Leagues

The 1994 Strike

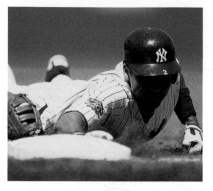

Hustle and hard work were values Jeter brought with him from the minor leagues.

games. At times, Jeter was afraid to have balls hit to him. "Still, you could tell it was there," says Yankees outfielder Shane Spencer, who spent the 1993 season in Greensboro. "You could see the greatness coming." Spencer wasn't the only one whom Jeter impressed. The South Atlantic League's managers named him the circuit's most outstanding major league prospect.

Despite the honor, the Yankees were still concerned about Jeter's fielding. So, in the spring of 1994, they sent him back to Tampa. Even though he had played well in the Instructional League in Florida the previous fall, making just one error in twenty games, the Yanks didn't want to hurry him and pay a price later. Jeter, however, had different plans. He tore up the Florida League, hitting .329, so New York sent him to Albany, its Class AA affiliate.

The jump in competition didn't bother Jeter at all. He was ready to shine, and proved it by hitting .377 in thirty-four games. More importantly, he was smooth and successful in the field. It was all coming together. The Yankees promoted him to Columbus of the

International League, their top minor-league club.

In one season, he had gone from the bottom of the minor leagues to the top, and everybody in the organization knew he was destined for big things, including Yankees owner George Steinbrenner.

"We'll be patient with him," Steinbrenner said. "Every year you look for Derek Jeter to stumble, and he just doesn't. He dominated rookie ball, so we moved him to [Class] A, and he dominated there. We sent him to double A, and he dominated there. At Columbus, it was the same thing. I'm telling you, he could be one of the special ones."

Jeter's friendship with teammate Jorge Posada started in the minor leagues. Here, Jeter and Posada are shown with the Toronto Blue Jays' Carlos Delgado at the 2000 All-Star Game.

The 1994 season ended with a work stoppage that cancelled the World Series. But it culminated with Jeter hitting .349 in thirty-five games. The following year, he hit .317 at Columbus, and though the error bug bit him again—he had 29—the Yankees didn't care.

> **"Every year you look for Derek Jeter to stumble, and he just doesn't."**
> **—George Steinbrenner**

They brought him up in September 1995, when the major-league *rosters* expanded from twenty-five to forty. There was Jeter, living across the river in New Jersey, eating at the same Bennigan's restaurant after every game with teammate and fellow call-up Jorge Posada, and wearing the Yankees' pinstripes.

"We were just little kids," Posada said. "We kept telling each other, 'Man, this is the big leagues, this is unbelievable. We gotta get here, and next time, we gotta stay.'"

Jeter stayed, all right. Did he ever.

There was no question who the Yankees' starting
shortstop would be in 1996: Derek Jeter!

CHAPTER FOUR

In the Big Leagues

When the 1996 season dawned, there were no more minor-league assignments or debates about where the best place for Jeter would be. He was the Yankees' starting shortstop, and it seemed just right.

The Yankees hadn't had a rookie at short on opening day since Tom Tresh in 1962. But Jeter didn't waste any time proving manager Joe Torre had made the correct decision. In a scene right out of Hollywood, Jeter hit his first big-league home run in New York's first game of the 1996 season, a solo shot off Cleveland Indians starting pitcher Dennis Martinez on April 2. From that moment on, he would be a fixture at the position. And everybody was impressed.

"It took me a while to adjust [to the big leagues], but he [Jeter] did it right away," said then Yankees first baseman Tino Martinez, who now plays with the St. Louis Cardinals.

Former Yankees pitcher Jimmy Key agreed. "His [Jeter's] best asset is his head."

Even though Jeter hit .306 in four minor-league seasons, many believed he would have to make a big adjustment to playing with the club. After all, this wasn't Columbus in Class AAA ball or even another, less-storied major-league team. This was the Yankees.

★ The Yankee Tradition

Jeter's dream came true when he learned he would be playing ball in historic Yankee Stadium.

The Stadium. The Big Apple. Jeter's response?

"I didn't expect to do anything different than I did in the minors," Derek said.

Jeter hit .314 his rookie year and led the Yankees in games played (157). He had 10 homers, 78 runs batted in (RBIs), and 25 doubles, and tied Martinez for the team lead in multihit games (49). From September 7 to September 25, Jeter hit in 17 straight games. He won the Rookie of the Year award in a landslide, and was even better in the playoffs, hitting .361 as the Yankees won their first world championship since 1978. It was a whirlwind year, one that Jeter handled with the class and composure of a veteran.

Derek was named the 1996 American League Rookie of the Year.

"The thing that sets Jeter apart is that he's not afraid to fail," former Yankees third baseman Charlie Hayes said in 1996. "He wants the ball hit to him in the last inning of the last game, with the whole World Series at stake."

Jeter may have seemed calm on the exterior, but he admitted to feeling butterflies, "especially while I'm waiting for the game to start." But he never looked frazzled. At the plate, he was patient and productive. Here he was, just twenty-two years old, playing on baseball's grandest stage, under the hottest, brightest lights, and he acted no differently from the way he had in high school. He played aggressively. He played to win. Jeter made mistakes, but he kept working.

"The first time I saw Derek Jeter play was in the spring of 1996," Joe Torre said. "Until then, I'd only heard about this young shortstop who wasn't much of a hitter and was a little raw defensively. But ready or not, he was getting his shot. The organization was committed to him.

"There was a presence about him that led me to believe he was going to develop quickly as a big leaguer."
—Joe Torre

Yankees manager Joe Torre (left) high-fives shortstop Derek Jeter.

"My initial evaluation? Certainly, Derek had a strong arm, and he was confident charging the ball. That was unusual for a kid that young. As I soon learned, though, he had a maturity unlike any other twenty-one-year-old I'd ever seen. There was a presence about him that led me to believe he was going to develop quickly as a big leaguer."

The day before Game 1 of the 1996 World Series against Atlanta, Jeter had a chance meeting with former Yankee great Dave Winfield, the man the young shortstop had idolized while growing up. The man whose poster was on his bedroom wall. But Jeter didn't dissolve into a puddle of nerves. He shook Winfield's hand, accepted a few words of encouragement, and went to work. He may have been excited, but nobody could tell.

"He's like someone who's thirty, thirty-two, a guy who's played eight, nine years,"

The New York Yankees won the World Series in 1996, and Jeter was thrilled to be part of the championship team. Here, he congratulates teammate Bernie Williams after a big hit.

Yankees pitching coach Mel Stottlemyre said of the then twenty-one-year-old Jeter.

When the season was all over, and Jeter had a chance to reflect, his cool deserted him. "It's like everything happened so fast," he said. "My first year, everything happened. We won the World Series, rookie of the year, everything came so quick. It was like everything's been in fast-forward. It's overwhelming."

Things continued on the same dizzying path in Jeter's second full year in the majors. Although his batting average slipped a bit, to .291 in 1997, Jeter remained a stalwart member of the Yankees. He led the American League with 748 plate appearances, and finished third in the league with 190 hits. Jeter scored 116 runs (fourth in the league), a feat that allowed him to be the first Yankee to score more than 100 runs in his first two seasons since the great Joe DiMaggio did it in 1936–1937. And, again, he was even better in the postseason, hitting .333 with two homers in the playoff series with Cleveland. If anybody felt Derek Jeter was a one-year wonder, his sophomore season proved otherwise. He was a rising star.

Still, Jeter didn't want to rest on his accomplishments. There was more to do; there were improvements to be made. The past had been great. The future could be greater.

"I can always get better," he said.

And he would.

Opposing teams soon learned to fear Derek Jeter at the plate, thanks to his powerful hitting.

CHAPTER FIVE

Superstardom

It was a familiar scene: Derek Jeter was tearing it up at Turner Field. Three at-bats. Three hits. Braves fans were no doubt averting their eyes. It was business as usual for the Yankees' star shortstop.

Only this time, instead of the World Series, Jeter was in Atlanta for the 2000 *All-Star Game*. And instead of doing his damage on behalf of the Bronx Bombers, he was leading the American League to its fourth straight Midsummer's Classic win and its tenth in its last thirteen games.

Less than a year after helping the Yanks win the 1999 World Series Championship against the Braves—with a .353 average in the Series—Jeter was back in Atlanta, spraying line drives everywhere. He had already returned once during the 2000 season, during *interleague play*, and had tied a career high with four hits in one game against the Braves. But this was bigger. With the entire baseball world tuned in, Jeter went three for three, with a two-run single, in the American League's 6–3 win.

"That really is a shocker," Atlanta shortstop Chipper Jones said after the game, joking about Jeter's great performance. "It's good to see no one else in the National League can get him out, either."

Jeter shows his agility and grace by leaping over an oncoming base runner.

Jeter wasn't even supposed to start the game. His good pal, Seattle shortstop Alex Rodriguez, had been voted in by the fans, but an injury had sidelined "A-Rod." So Jeter stepped in. And stole the show. He had a first-inning double off Arizona's Randy Johnson and then singled and scored in the third against Kevin Brown of the Dodgers. In the fourth, Jeter hit a big two-run single off the Mets' Al Leiter. Three of the best pitchers the National League had to offer couldn't get him out. "He's a great hitter," said Johnson, who retired the other three hitters he faced in seven pitches.

In just his fifth big-league season, Derek Jeter had risen to superstar status. The 2000 All-Star Game was just one more brilliant chapter in his brief but prosperous career. His performance made him the first Yankee ever to win the game's Most Valuable Player award. Babe Ruth, Lou Gehrig, Joe DiMaggio, Mickey Mantle, and scores of other Yanks had

played in the game, but none had done what Jeter had.

"It's good for Derek, just another thing for his resume," said Jorge Posada. "He's getting better. He's twenty-six years old and just getting better and better."

Jeter's first two years in the majors were hugely successful. He was named Rookie of the Year and earned a World Series ring. But they were just appetizers. Jeter blossomed into a marquee player in 1998, posting career highs in average (.324), runs (127), RBIs (84), stolen bases (30), slugging percentage (.481), and hits (203) for a Yankees team that won 114 games during the regular season and then cruised through the playoffs and the World Series. It was

"He's a rock star. He's whatever makes the girls swoon and the guys jealous."

—Joe Torre

How sweet it is! Jeter and manager Joe Torre celebrate a win over the Oakland Athletics in the 2000 Division Series.

considered one of the greatest clubs in baseball history, and Jeter was a key cog in the machine. His nineteen home runs set a record for Yankees shortstops. He had a fifteen-game hitting streak, was named the American League's Player of the Month for August, and earned his first All-Star Game invite.

His success earned him the respect of teammates and opponents and considerable attention from the media. But Jeter was becoming more than just a great baseball player. He was a full-fledged phenomenon, as coveted for his good looks and smooth personality as for his hot bat and glove.

"Going around New York, he's a matinee idol, there's no question," Yankees manager Joe Torre said. "He's a rock star. He's whatever makes the girls swoon and the guys jealous."

"It's kind of like Elvis a little bit," former teammate Scott Brosius said, laughing.

Jeter wasn't trying to set the town on fire. He was a young man trying to get better in his profession and enjoy himself off the field. It was clear he was doing both. It seemed as if he had everything in perfect order. His play was getting better every year. His social life was rocking. And through his Turn 2 Foundation, for which his father serves as executive director, Jeter was giving back to the community, raising money for organizations—the Boys Club of America and others—that help keep kids away from drugs and alcohol.

"It's an issue that faces everyone, regardless of race, whether you're black or white, Spanish, or where you grew up, or whether you were rich or poor," Jeter said of substance abuse. "So, I think it's a great cause."

Jeter's big heart off the field didn't show up when he was at the plate. He wasn't about to give anybody a break. It didn't matter which pitcher he was facing, he was coming after him—usually with great results. In 1999, Jeter hit .349, with 219 hits, 24 home runs, 102 RBIs, 134 runs scored, 37 doubles, and 9 triples—all career highs. He also picked up his third World Series championship in four years, and continued to earn the respect of those he faced.

"You can throw him inside as much as you want, and he can still fist the ball off," then Orioles relief pitcher Jesse Orosco said. "You can throw the ball low and away, and he can hit with power the other way. We have pitchers' meetings, and he's one of those guys where you just stay on the subject for a while. What do you do?"

While the rest of the baseball world tried to figure that out, Jeter just kept rolling along, piling up championship rings and statistics.

And smiling all the while.

Happiness is winning big. Derek Jeter is swarmed by teammates after another big Yankees victory.

Jeter's continued success earned him his teammates' approval and a big contract from the Yankees.

CHAPTER SIX

Above and Beyond

A few months before the 2001 season began, Alex Rodriguez and the Texas Rangers rocked the sporting world.

Ten years, $252 million. Amazing.

A-Rod had left Seattle for the biggest, fattest contract in professional sports history. All future deals would be measured by his—including Jeter's. Jeter had come close to signing a giant contract of his own before the 2000 season, when his agent, Casey Close, agreed on a seven-year, $118.5 million package with team representatives. But Yankees owner George Steinbrenner overruled everybody. He didn't want to set a salary record, and he decided to wait until some other stars, including A-Rod, signed.

Once that deal was done, it was time to pay Jeter. The result, which was agreed upon in February 2001, was a ten-year, $189 million contract that included a $16 million signing bonus. It would keep him in pinstripes through the entire prime of his career and made him the third-highest-paid player in the game, behind A-Rod and Boston outfielder Manny Ramirez. In typical fashion, Jeter didn't care one bit that there were others with fatter checkbooks than him.

> **"Being the highest paid is not something I covet."**
> **—Derek Jeter**

"Being the highest paid is not something I covet," Jeter said at the press conference announcing the deal. "If that was the case, I would have waited another year and maximized my earning potential, so to speak."

He was right. Jeter actually signed with the Yankees a year before he was eligible to be a *free agent*. But it didn't matter to him whether he would average $19 million or $59 million a year. He was staying with the team he loved for at least ten more years. He would have a chance to have his number retired by the world's most famous franchise, joining greats like Babe Ruth, Lou Gehrig, and Joe DiMaggio. Jeter had even insisted on a contract clause that prohibited the Yankees from trading him without his permission. He wasn't going anywhere.

"I couldn't picture it," he said. "I really felt there was no reason to see if the grass was greener on the other side. Even if I had played out the year, my first choice would have been New York.

"I never intended to play elsewhere, and to be honest with you, never intended to look elsewhere."

The Yankees were thrilled he felt that way, because Jeter had become the team's leader, despite being younger than many of his teammates. He finished the 2000 season with a club-best .339 average, 15 homers and 73 *RBIs*. New York again won the World Series, beating the Mets in New York's first *Subway Series* in forty-four years. And Jeter was the series *MVP*. In his five full

By the 2002 season, Derek Jeter had become a fixture on the American League All-Star roster.

major-league seasons, the Yankees had won the four championships, and he had become one of baseball's biggest stars.

But New York fans would have to wait to welcome Jeter to the 2001 season. A strained right quadriceps, suffered during spring train-ing, landed him on the fifteen-day disabled list. It wasn't a crippling injury, but it was enough to keep him out of the lineup for sev-eral games. Although Jeter wanted to play, he admitted he felt pain when he ran. With a long regular season and the playoffs looming, the Yankees wanted to be safe.

Yankees manager Joe Torre and Arizona skipper Bob Brenly greet President George W. Bush before Game 3 of the 2001 World Series in New York. President Bush threw out the ceremonial first pitch.

"I know he probably could go out and play, but again, because it's such a short time being away, you really have to look at the big picture," Yankees manager Joe Torre said. "He did not try to talk me out of it. Once I said this is what I want to do, that was it."

So, while the Yankees headed north from their Fort Lauderdale, Florida, training site, Jeter stayed behind, playing in minor-league *exhibition games* and trying to get his leg healthy. He did just that. By the time Jeter joined the Yankees, he was ready for another big year. And he delivered, hitting .311, with 21 homers and 74 RBIs. Yet, despite the new contract and the hysteria that continued to surround him, Jeter remained focused on his job.

"It's the same Derek Jeter," Torre said. "He's doing the same things he always did, just more of it. He's a very confident young man, and he has the wherewithal to back it up. And he's not caught up in his celebrity or stardom. He knows what comes first."

Jeter and Yankees coach Willie Randolph observe a moment of silence before a game against Chicago on September 19, 2001, just days after the September 11 terrorist attacks.

Jeter knew what came last, too—the World Series. The Yankees would be meeting Arizona for the title, trying to win their fourth straight championship and the fifth during Jeter's six years with the team.

And then came September 11, 2001. In the wake of the horrible terrorist attacks of September 11, the city searched for something to rally around. New York sure needed the diversion. The Yankees provided the opportunity, bringing New Yorkers together with another great postseason run. Even New York Mets fans were on the bandwagon. And when President George W. Bush threw out the first pitch before Game 3 in New York, it seemed as if the city were on its way back.

The Yankees responded with the kind of dramatic play never before seen on baseball's biggest stage. Twice they found themselves down, with two outs in the ninth inning. Twice they rallied for victory. In the fourth game, first baseman Tino Martinez crushed a two-out, three-run homer to tie the score. Jeter won it in the tenth inning with a home run of his own. One night later, third baseman Scott Brosius's two-run homer gave the Yanks another improbable win.

But New York couldn't make the magic last. The Diamondbacks rallied from the crushing defeat to win twice at home, using a little late magic of their own to secure the championship. Luis Gonzalez's ninth-inning bloop

"I don't think you ever sit around and say you're good, until you hit a thousand with no errors."

—Derek Jeter

single—just over Jeter's outstretched glove—gave Arizona the championship. It was a bitter loss for the Yankees, and for New York.

The off-season was filled with activity, as the team turned over its roster, adding Oakland slugger Jason Giambi, in an attempt to win it all again in 2002. Jeter went quietly on his way, making his usual off-season preparations for the coming season. He hosted *Saturday Night Live* and showed that his style and grace on the field translated to the stage. He continued to enjoy his life in New York, but he knew that his journey wasn't finished.

"I don't think you ever sit around and say you're good, until you hit a thousand with no errors," he said. "You still have something to work on, and there's always aspects to the game that you can try and improve, whether it is offense, defense, baserunning or whatever. And I don't think you can ever be content with how you play. Otherwise, you are not going to improve."

Derek Jeter is going to get better. But don't expect him to brag about his accomplishments or forget the hard work that got him to the top. He'll continue to hustle, to smile for the cameras, and to sign for the fans. Some players may refuse to do all that, but not Jeter.

It's all part of the dream.

It hasn't been all smiles for Jeter. Here, he sits in the dugout after the Yankees' loss to Arizona in the 2002 World Series.

stats

Stats

Derek Jeter

Born: June 26, 19

GLOSSARY

All-Star Game—The All-Star Game is an annual July contest between the best players from the National and American Leagues. The first All-Star Game was played in 1933.

American League (National League)—Baseball is divided into two separate groups of teams, the National and American Leagues. Each year, the champions of each league meet in the World Series to determine the best team in baseball. The Yankees are in the American League.

cutoff man—Because it's hard to make a throw from deep in the outfield all the way to home plate or third base, a fielder will often throw the ball to a teammate, the cutoff man, who will then throw to home plate or another base to try to get a runner out.

dynasty—A period during which a certain team dominates play in a sport. Because the Yankees have won so many World Series championships, including four in the last six years, they are considered a dynasty.

exhibition games—Baseball contests played during the late winter and early spring to allow players to prepare for the season. Although scores and statistics are kept, the games don't count in the standings.

free agent—A player who is no longer tied by contract to any one team and is free to negotiate with any baseball club.

interleague play—Regular-season games played between teams of the National and American Leagues. Before instituted in 1997, the only time teams from the two leagues met was in the World Series.

MVP (Most Valuable Player)—The player deemed to be most instrumental in his team's success. This award is given each year to a worthy player from each league.

roster—The list of players on any given team.

RBI (Runs Batted In)—A statistic of how many baserunners reach home on a hit by a particular batter, or when the batter is issued on a walk when the bases are full.

Subway Series—A World Series involving two teams from New York. Fans would be able to get to games in each team's stadium by taking the subway. The first Subway Series was played between the Yankees and the Brooklyn Dodgers in 1941. The Yankees and New York Mets played the most recent Subway Series in 2000.

walk—To advance to first base as a result of being thrown four pitches out of the strike zone (balls), as ruled by the umpire.

World Series—The annual October contest between the champions of the American and National Leagues to determine Major League Baseball's best team. The clubs compete in a best-of-seven format, with the first team to win four games crowned champion.

Find Out More

Web Sites
The Turn 2 Foundation
P.O. Box 19158
Kalamazoo, MI 49019
http://www.turn2foundation.org

The Official Site of Major League Baseball
www.mlb.com

The Baseball Hall of Fame
www.baseballhalloffame.com

Books

Pietrusza, David. *The New York Yankees Baseball Team*. Berkeley Heights, NJ: Enslow
    Publishers, Inc. 1998.

Stewart, Mark. *Derek Jeter: Substance and Style*. Brookfield, CT: Millbrook Press Trade,
    1999.

Torres, John Albert. *Derek Jeter*. Bear, DE: Mitchell Lane Publishers, Inc., 2000.

INDEX
Page numbers for illustrations are in *bold face*.

age, 27–28, 33, 38
agent, 37
All-Star Games, 9, **23,** 31–32, 34, **38**
Arizona Diamondbacks, **39,** 40–41, **41**
Atlanta Braves, 31
awards, 16, 22, 26, **27,** 32–33, 34, 38

basketball, 14
batting average
calculating of, 15
   See also statistics
birth, 43
Boggs, Wade, 20–21
Brosius, Scott, 34, 40
Brown, Kevin, 32
Bush, President George W., **39,** 40

childhood, 9, 13–14
Cincinnati Reds, 16–17
Cleveland Indians, 25, 29
community service, 34–35
Cone, David, 10–11
contract, **36,** 37–38
Cooperstown Hall of Fame, 16, **17**
cutoff man, 8

Delgado, Carlos, **23**
disappointments, 19, 40–41, **41**
Division Series, **34**
draft, 16–17
drugs, 34–35

education
   academic, 14, 16–17
   baseball, 21–22
exhibition games, 39

family, 13–15, **15,** 34
fans, **10,** 10–11, 34
fielding, **2–3,** 8, **8, 20,** 21–22, **32–33,** 40–41
free agency, 38
friends, 15, 23, **23,** 32

Giambi, Jason, 41
Giambi, Jeremy, 7, 8
Gonzalez, Luis, 40–41
Groch, Dick, 17

Hayes, Charles, 27
heroes, 9, 16, 20–21, 28
high school sports, 15–16
hitting, **14,** 19, 22, 23, 25, 26, 29, **30,** 31–34, 35
   See also statistics

injuries, 39
Instructional League, 22
interleague play, 31

Johnson, Randy, 32
Jones, Chipper, 31

Key, Jimmy, 25

Larkin, Barry, 16
leagues, 45
Leiter, Al, 32
Little League, 14
Long, Terrence, 7

major leagues, **18**
   first experience, 20–21
   rookie year, 23–29, **24, 27,** 43
   second year, 29
   as star, 10–11, 31–39
Martinez, Dennis, 25
Martinez, Tino, 25, 40

Mattingly, Don, 20–21
minor leagues, 19–23, **20, 22,** 39
Mottola, Chad, 17
Mussina, Mike, 7
MVP (most valuable player), 32–33

number, 9, 38

Oakland Athletics, 7–9, **34**
Orosco, Jesse, 35

playoffs, **6,** 7–9, 26, 29, **34**
Posada, Jorge, 7, 8, 23, **23,** 33
position, 8, **8,** 16, **24,** 25, **32–33**

racism, 14–15
Ramirez, Manny, 37
RBIs (runs batted in), 26, 33, 35, 38
    See also statistics
records, 29, 34
right/left-handedness, 43
Rodriguez, Alex, 32, 37

September 11 2001 attack, 40, **40**
size, 9, 43
slugging percentage, 33
    See also statistics
Spencer, Shane, 8
spring training, 20–21, 39
stadium, **20, 26**
statistics, 33, 35, 38, 39
summary of, 43
Steinbrenner, George, 23, 37
Stottlemyre, Mel, 28–29
strikes (work stoppage), 22, 23
Subway Series, 38
television, 10, 41
Torre, Joe, 8, **27,** 27–28, 34, **34,** 39, **39**
trades, 38

Web sites, 10, 44
Williams, Bernie, **28**
Winfield, Dave, 28
World Series, 9, **9,** 26, **28,** 35, 38, **39,** 40–41, **41**
    See also playoffs

Yankees, **6,** 7, 13, 16–17, **18, 20,** 23, 26, **26,** 27, 33–34

PHOTO CREDITS

Photo research by Regina Flanagan.
Cover: John Williams, Major League Baseball Photos.
Title Page: Reuters NewMedia Inc./Corbis.
AP/Wide World Photos: 6,14, 18, 28, 30, 36; Major League
Baseball Photos: Rich Pilling: 8, 17, 22, 27 (top), 32-33;
Darren Carrol: 35; Sports Illustrated: Nitin Vadakul: 9;
Stephen Green: 10; Walter Iooss, Jr.: 11; Tom DiPace: 24; V.J.
Lovero: 20; Simon Bruty: 42; Reuters NewMedia Inc./Corbis: 12,
23, 40, 41; Corbis: John-Marshall Mantel: 15; Tannen
Maury/AFP: 38; Agence France Presse: Timothy A. Clary: 27;
John Mabanglo: 34; Luke Frazza: 39; Icon Sports Media: 20
(top), 26.